CZERNY

THE SCHOOL OF VELOCITY OPUS 299

EDITED BY WILLARD A. PALMER

About This Edition

Carl Czerny (1791–1857) was a pupil of Beethoven and the teacher of Liszt. He was one of the most sought-after piano teachers of his day and Beethoven regarded him highly enough to entrust his beloved nephew, Karl, to his pedagogy. Because Czerny was so prodigious in his understanding of the elements most important to the development of technical facility at the keyboard, his studies became standard during his lifetime, and he was very successful as a composer as well as a teacher.

Czerny's total number of works ran to Opus 1000 and hundreds of these were technical studies. Of these volumes, over a dozen are still in general use with Opus 299 retaining its lead as the most popular volume of piano studies ever written. Its usefulness in modern piano study is due to the fact that it offers practical training in well-articulated pianistic passagework, developing those characteristic motion-shapes with which the pianist must be most familiar, particularly in playing the virtuoso music of the Romantic period. In addition to this, each study is a complete musical composition, demanding attention to dynamics and phrasing as well as control of musical resources. The student who masters Opus 299 has indeed progressed a long way in the "school of velocity."

The present edition eliminates many unnecessary finger numbers but adds a few where they are needed. Indefinite dynamics have been clarified. The music is spaciously engraved for easier reading.

Second Edition
Copyright © 1992 by Alfred Music
All rights reserved. Produced in USA.

Cover art: Vienna, *viewed from the Belvedere*
by Bernardo Bellotto (Italian, 1720–1780)
Kunsthistorisches Museum, Vienna

Alfred has made every effort to make this book not only attractive but more useful and long-lasting as well. Usually, large books do not lie flat or stay open on the music rack. In addition, the pages (which are glued together) tend to break away from the spine after repeated use.

In this edition, pages are sewn together in multiples of 16. This special process prevents pages from falling out of the book while allowing it to stay open for ease in playing. We hope this unique binding will give you added pleasure and additional use.

2

The School of Velocity
Book One

Edited by
Willard A. Palmer

Carl Czerny Op. 299, Book 1

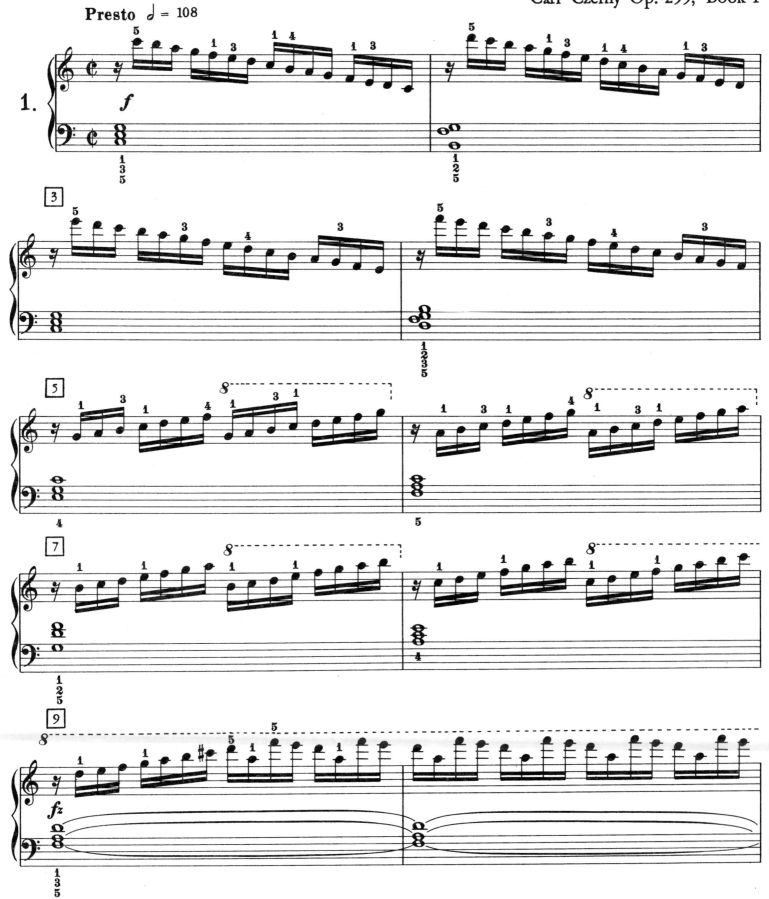

Copyright MCMLXIX by Alfred Music Co., Inc.

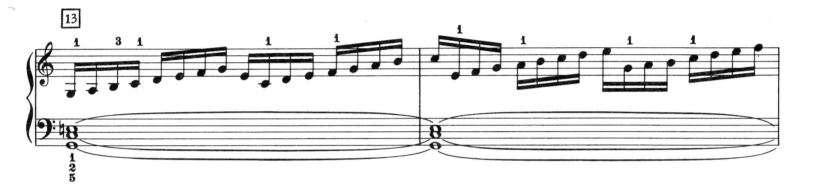

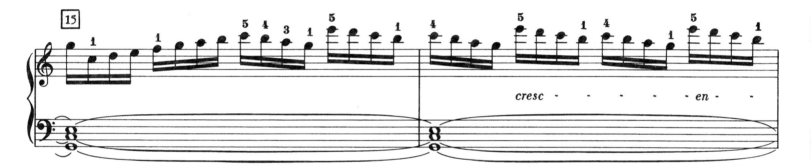

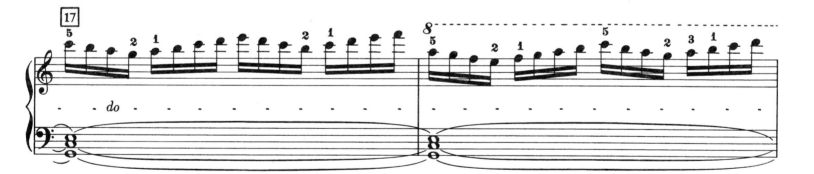

4

Molto Allegro ♩ = 104

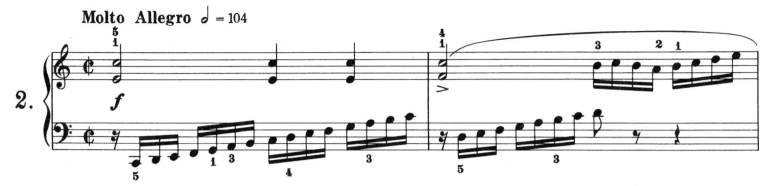

2.

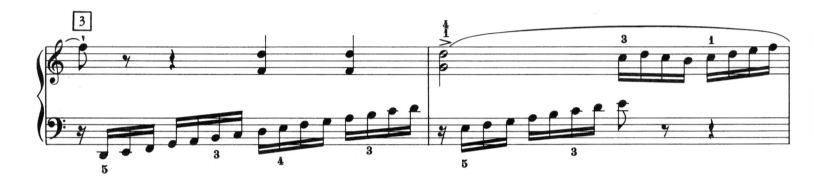

cresc. - - - - - - -

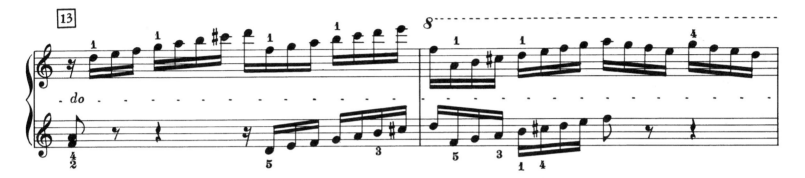

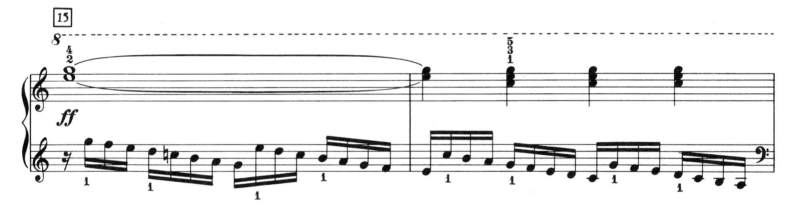

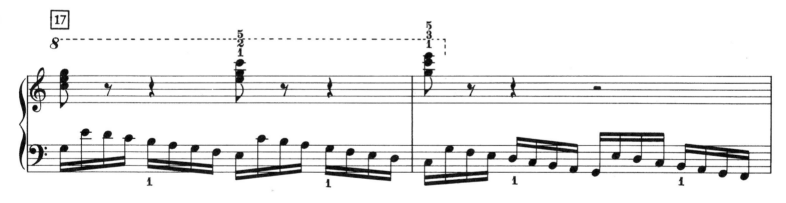

Presto ♩ = 108

3.

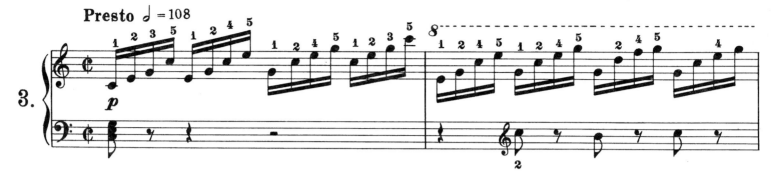

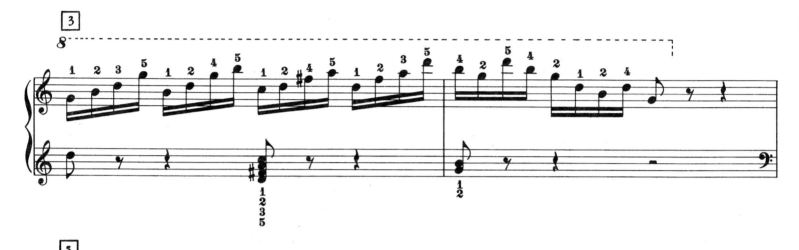

cresc - - - - - - - - - - - *en* - - -

8

Molto Allegro ♩=108

5.

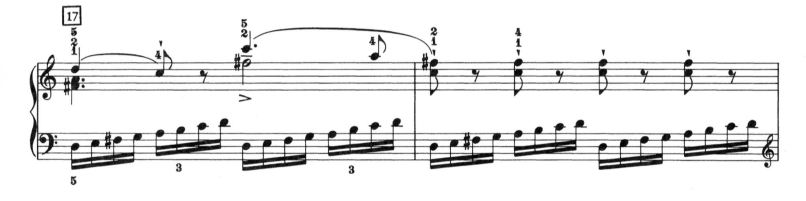

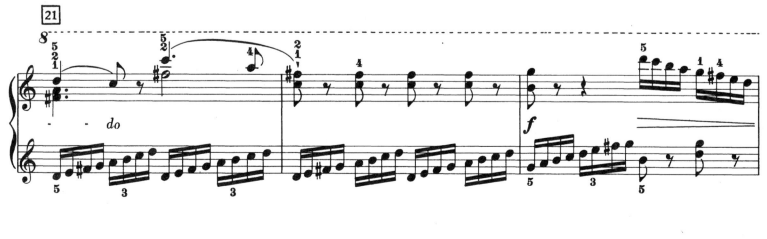

12

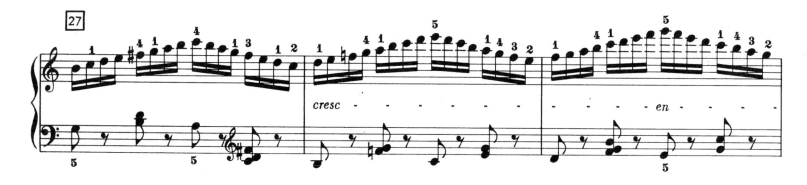

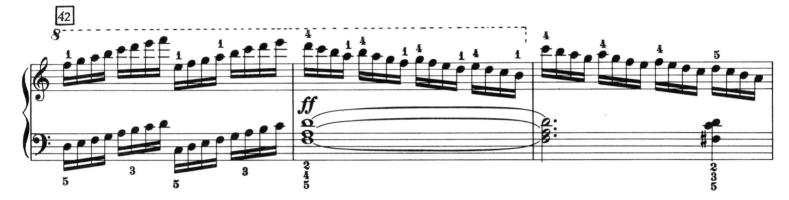

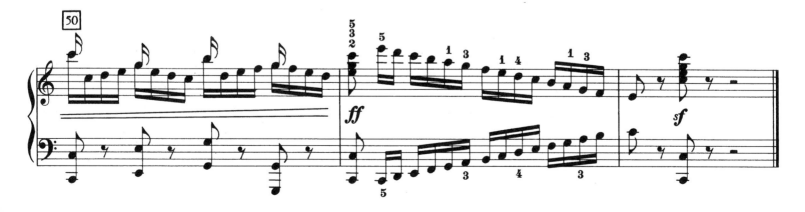

14

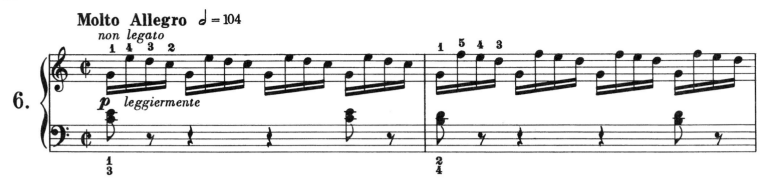

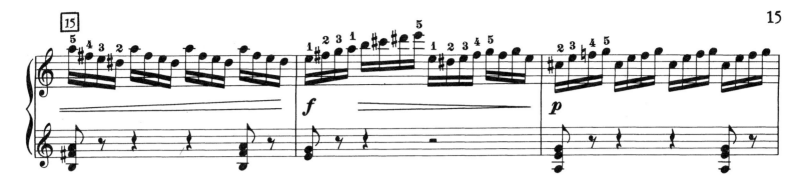

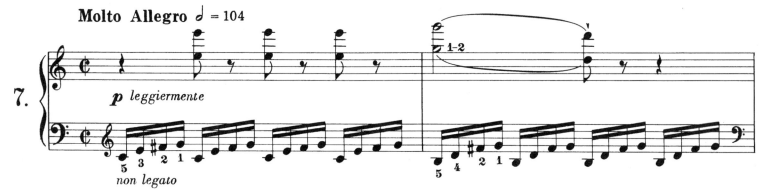

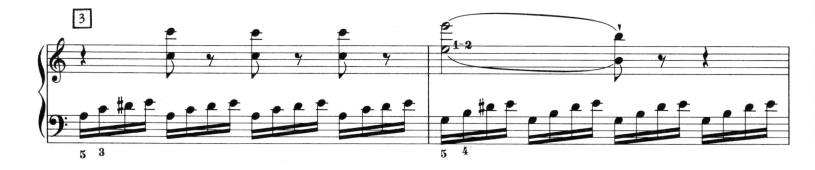

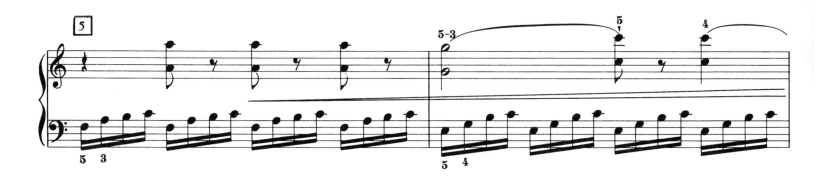

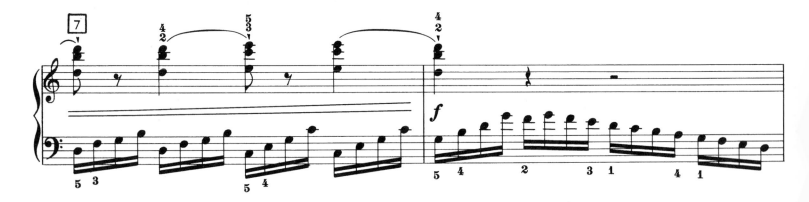

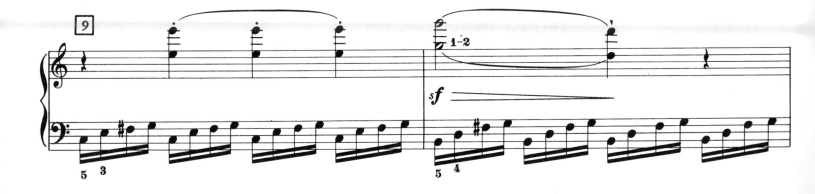

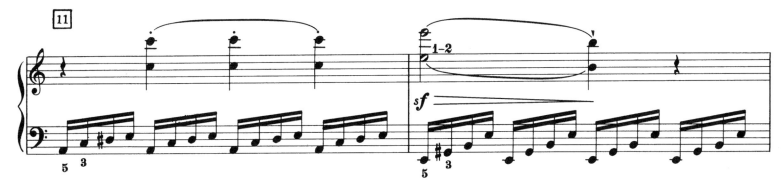

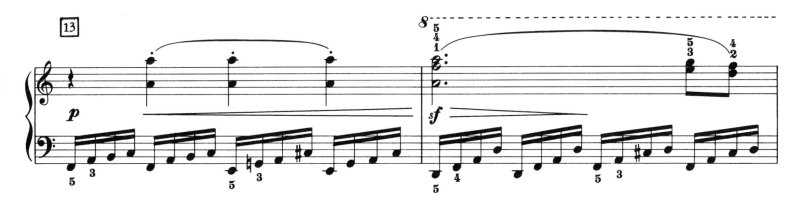

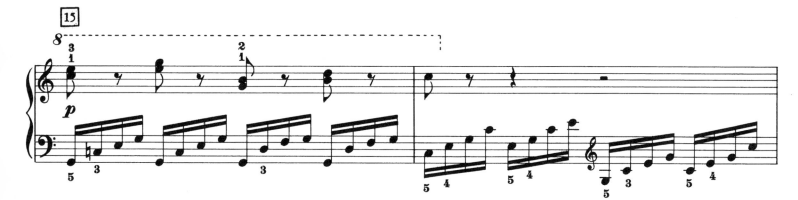

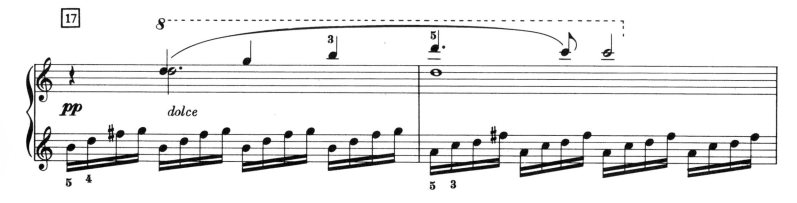

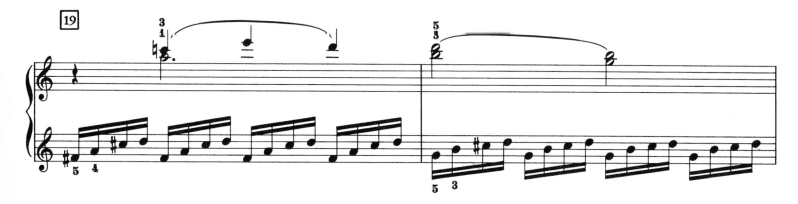

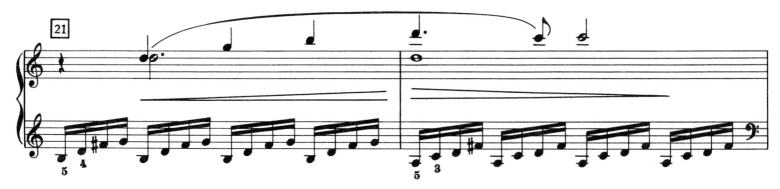

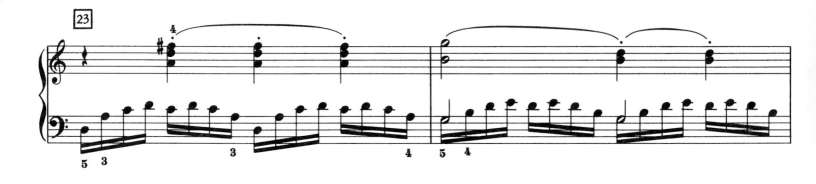

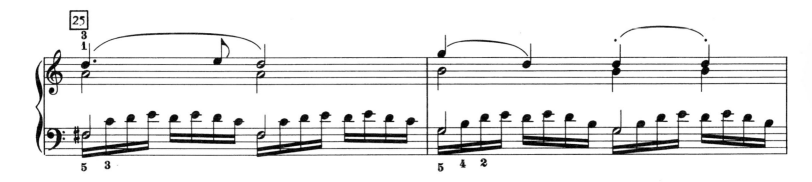

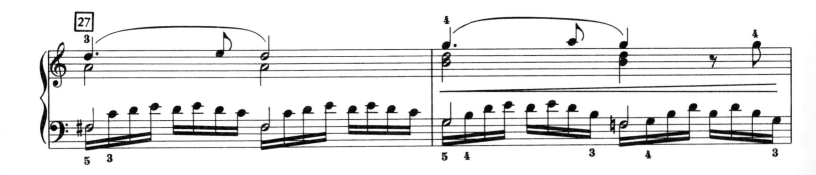

Molto Allegro ♩ = 104

8.

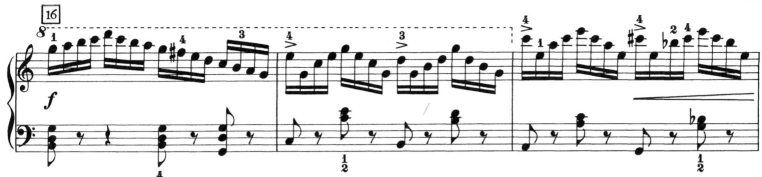

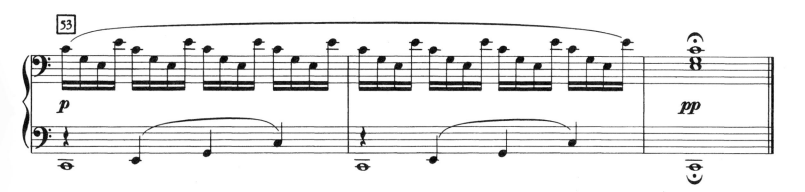

24

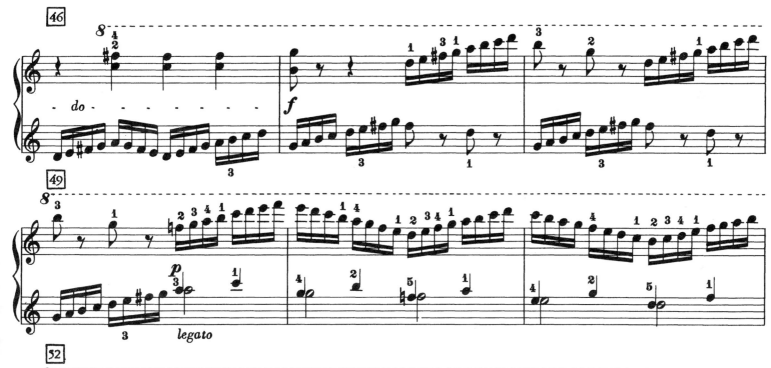

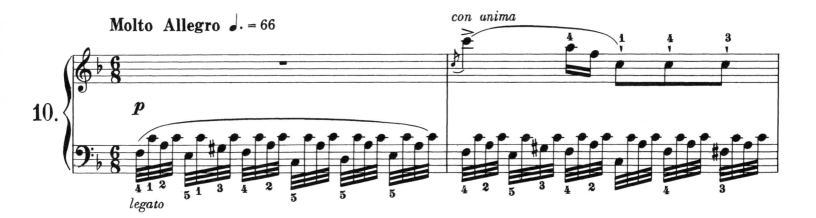

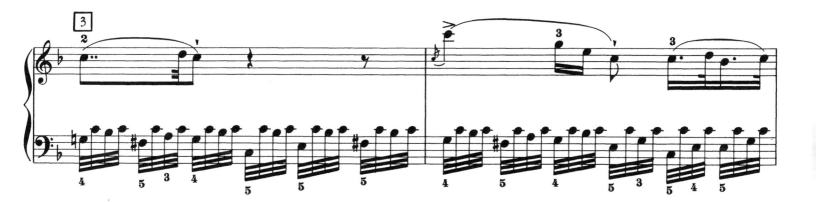

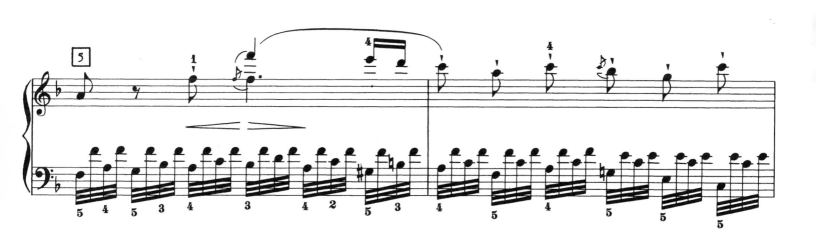

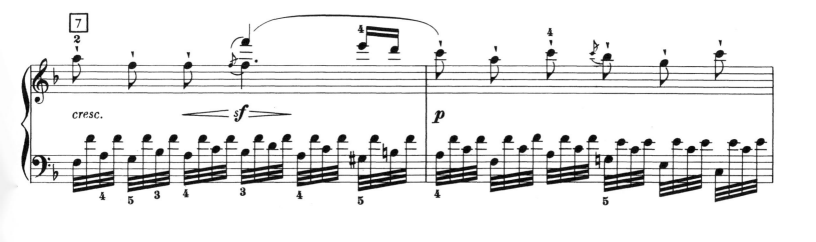

30

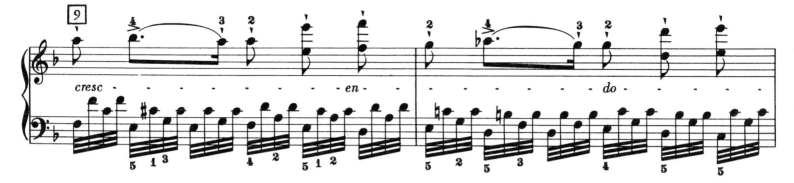

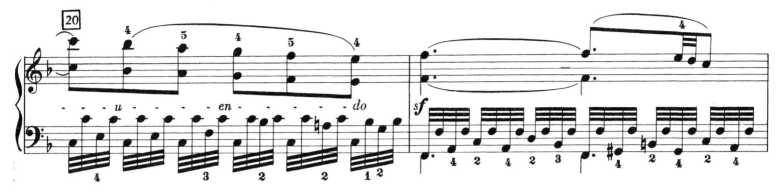

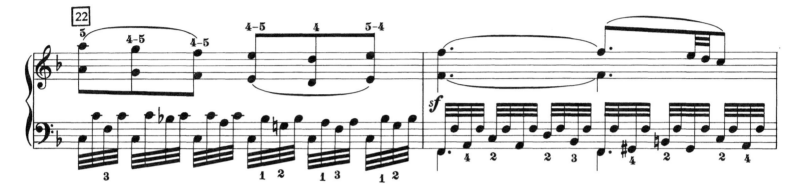

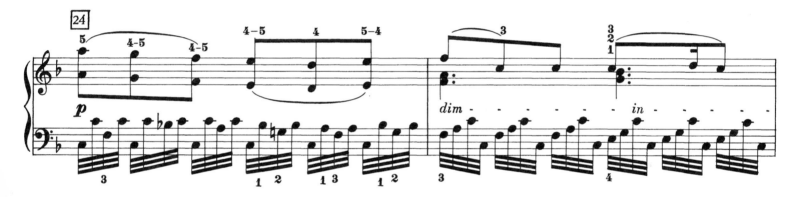

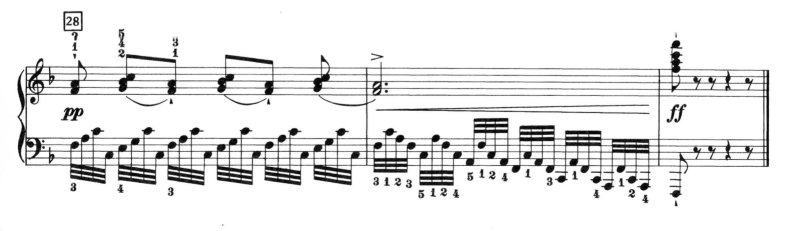

The School of Velocity

Book 2

Edited by
Willard A. Palmer

Carl Czerny Op. 299, Book 2

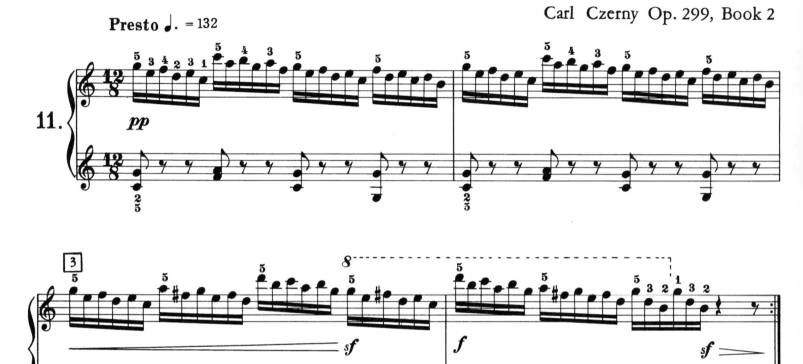

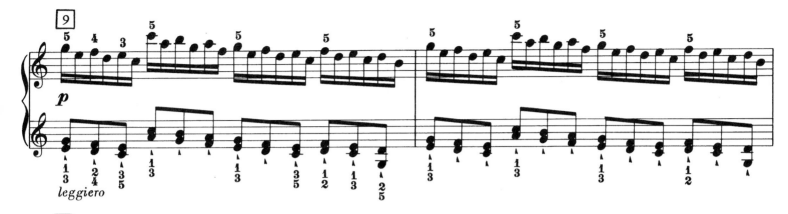

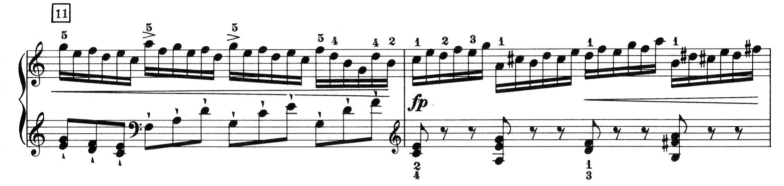

Molto Allegro $\quad \boldsymbol{\downarrow} = 92$

12.

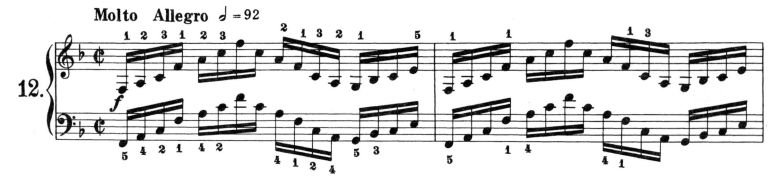

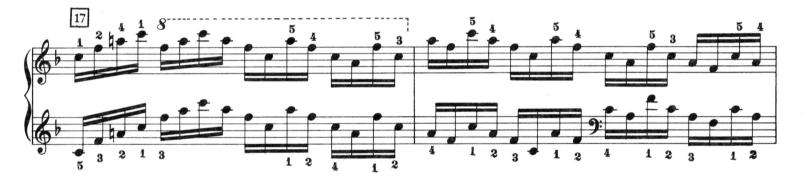

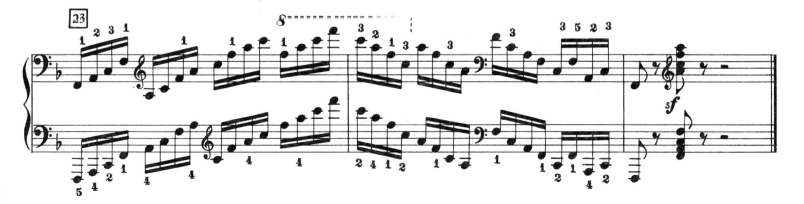

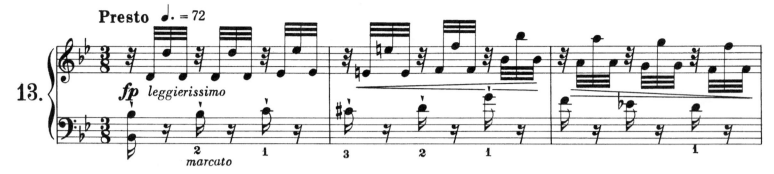

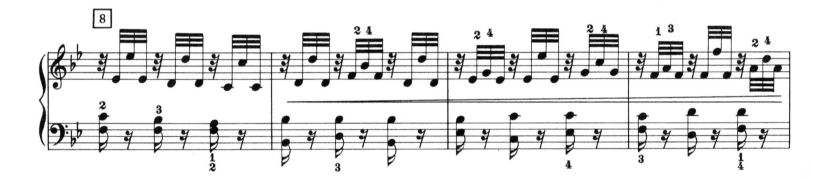

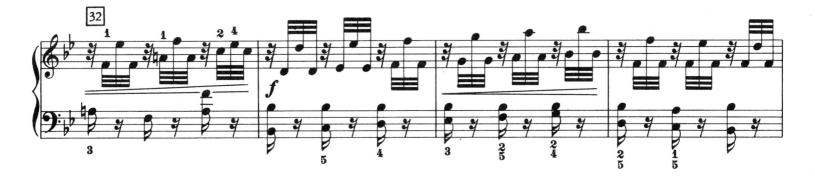

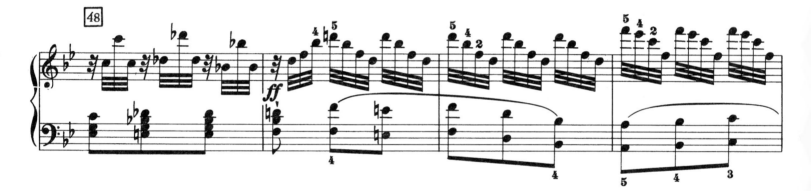

Molto vivo e velocissimo ♩ = 116

14.

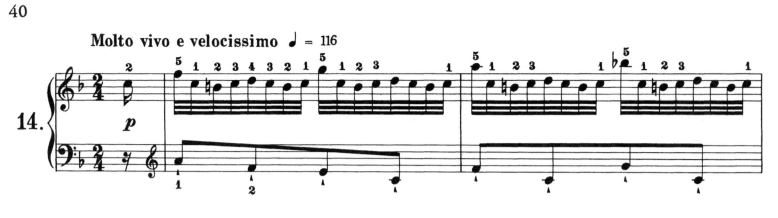

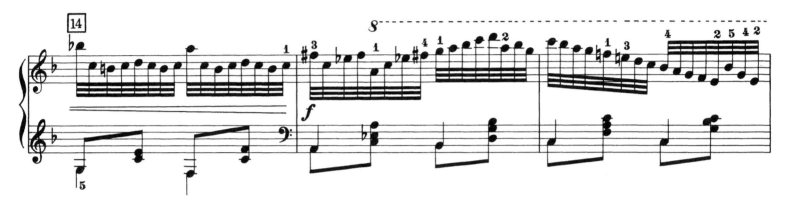

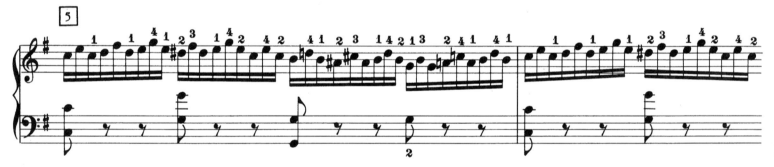

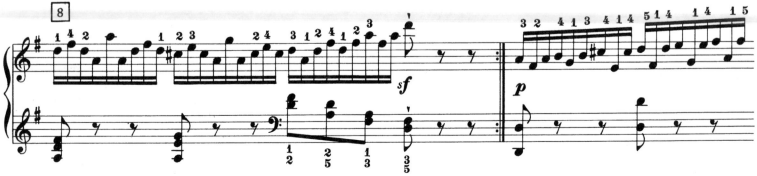

Molto Allegro ♩ = 96

17.

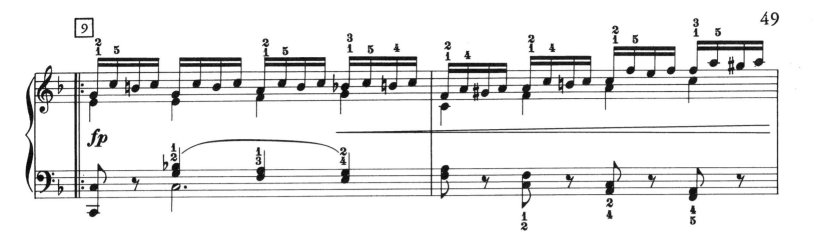

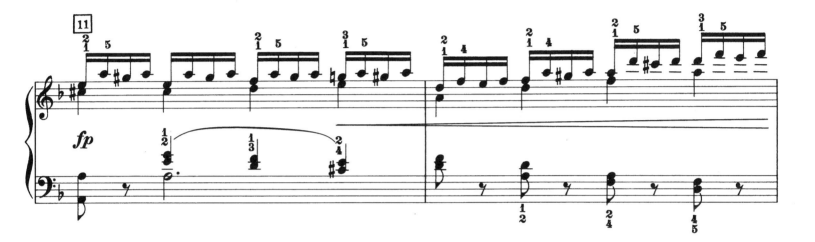

Molto Allegro ♩ = 120

18.

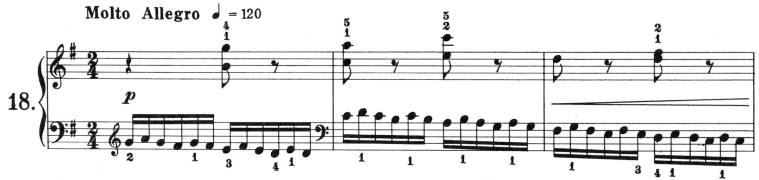

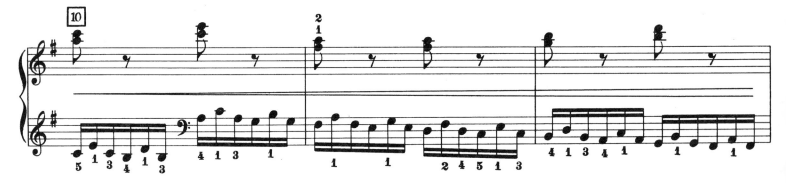

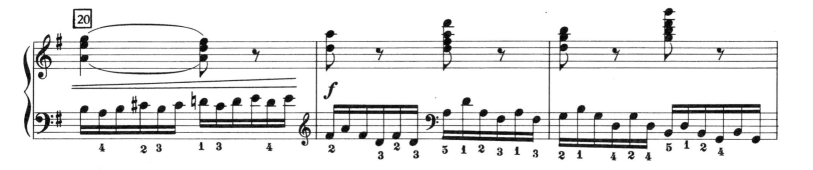

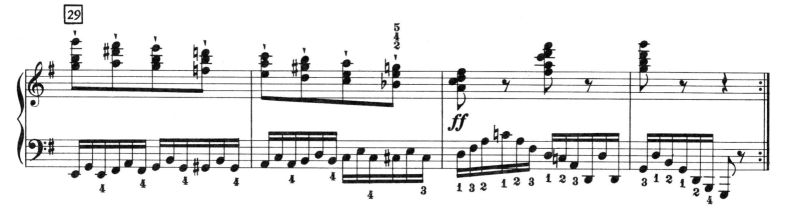

52

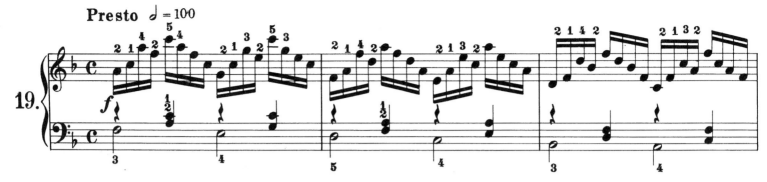

19.

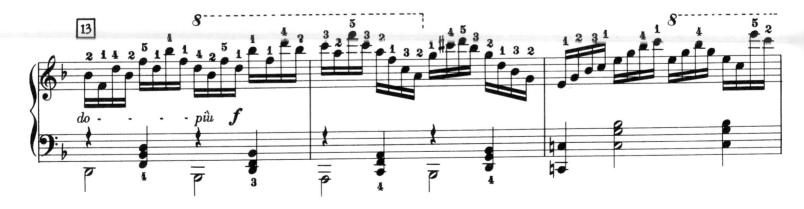

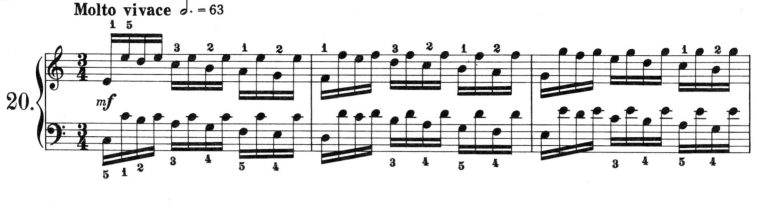

56

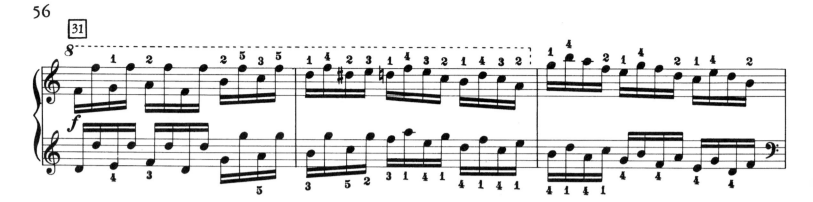

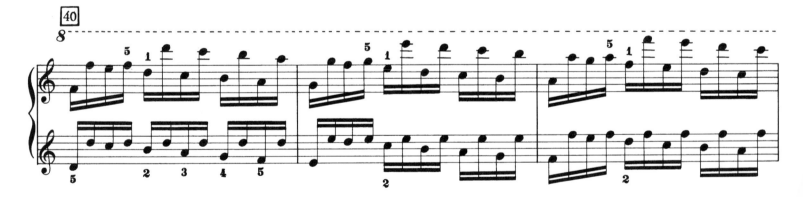

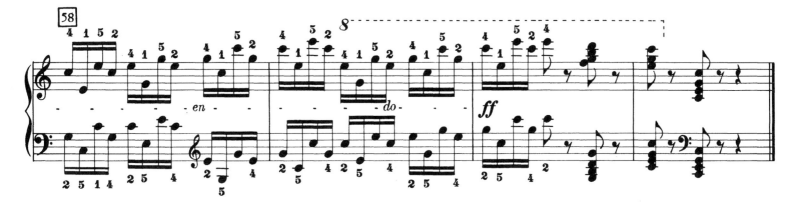

The School of Velocity

Book 3

Edited by
Willard A. Palmer

Carl Czerny Op. 299, Book 3

Molto Allegro ♩ = 104

21.

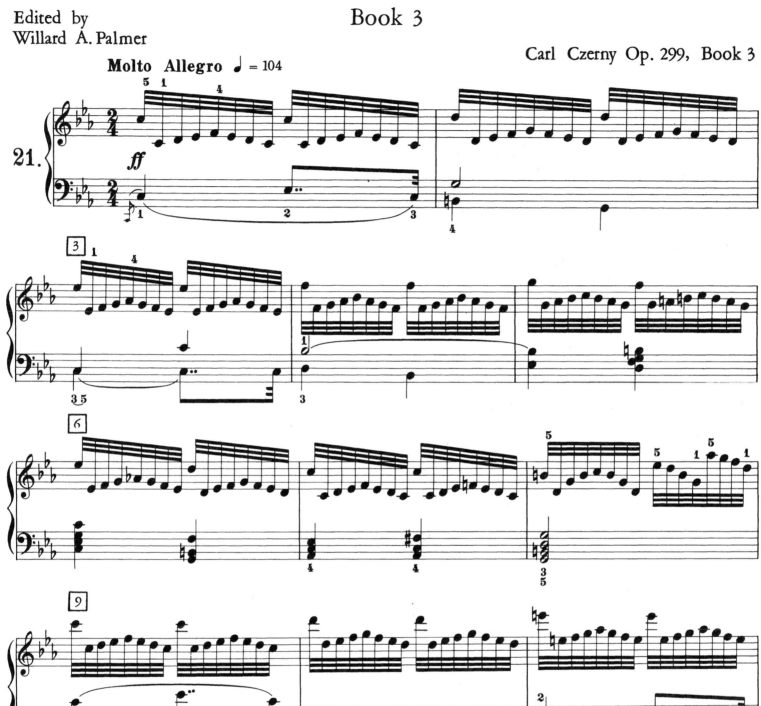

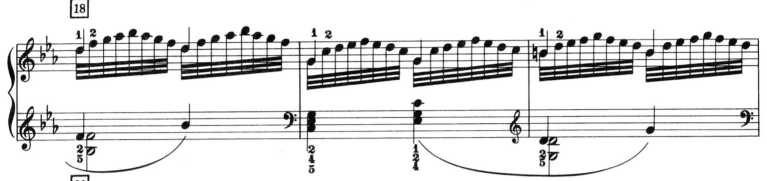

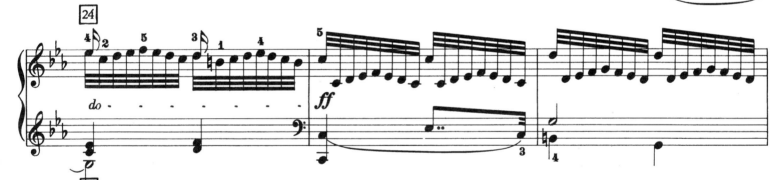

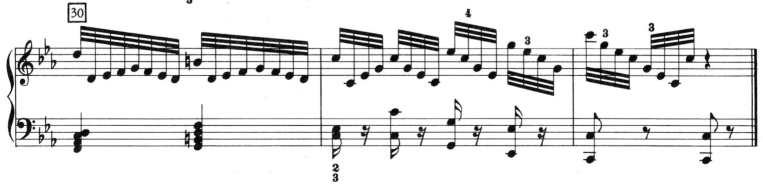

Molto Allegro ♩ = 96

sempre simile

22.

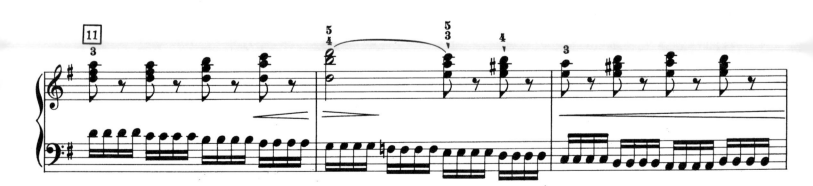

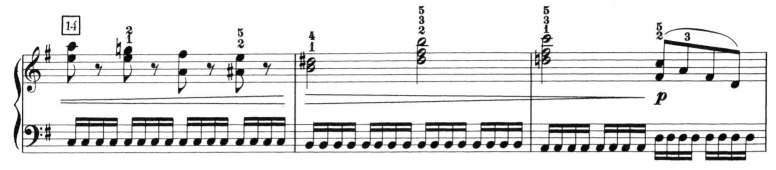

62

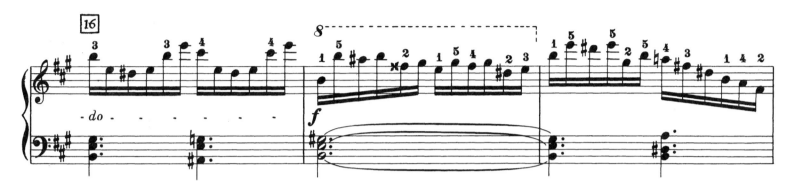

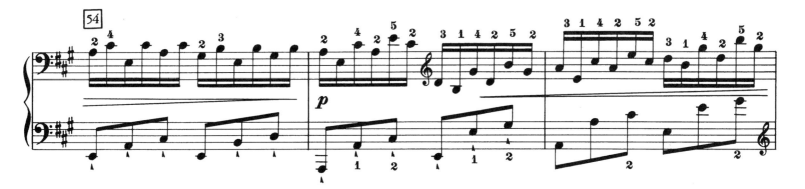

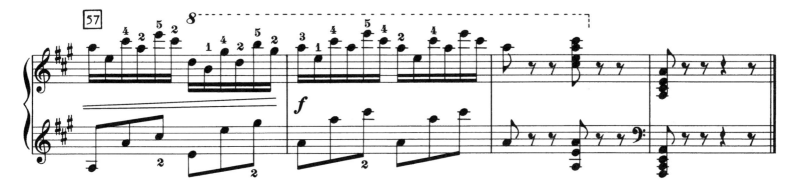

Molto Allegro ♩ = 108

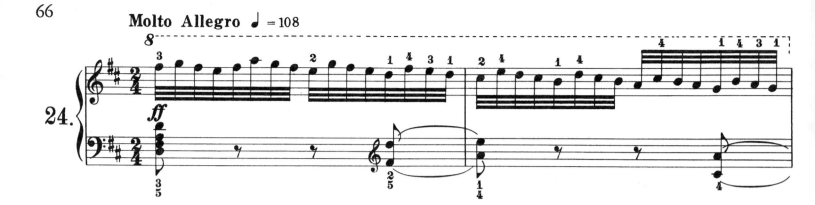

24.

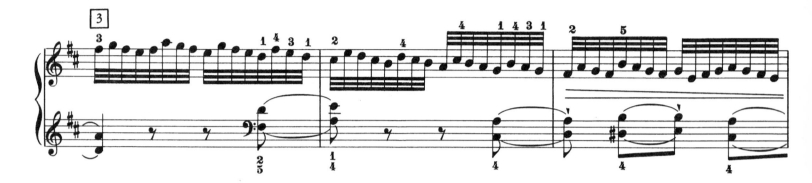

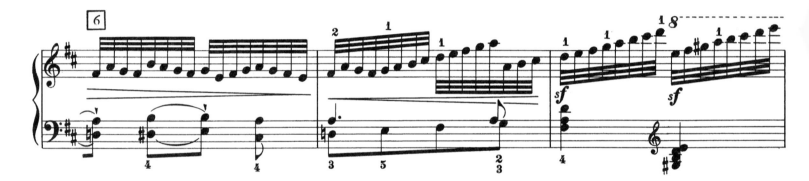

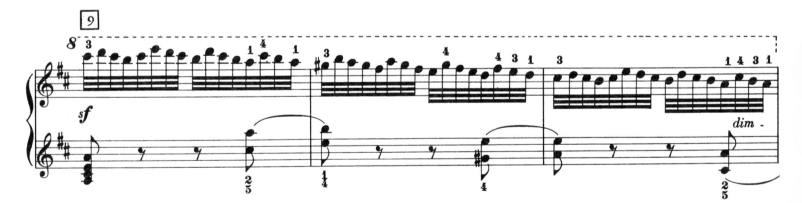

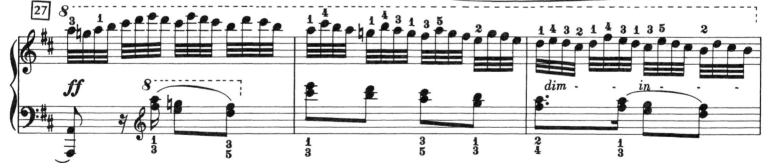

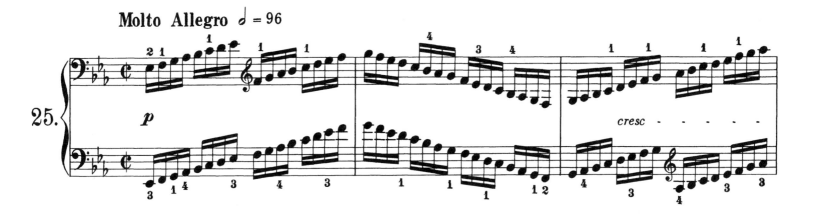

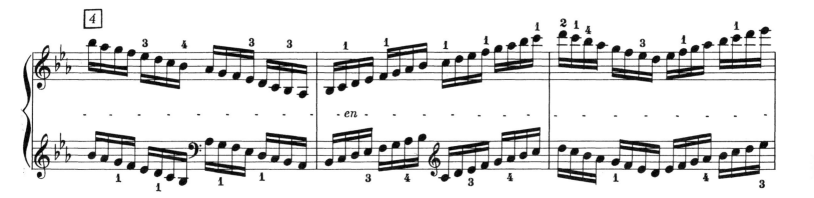

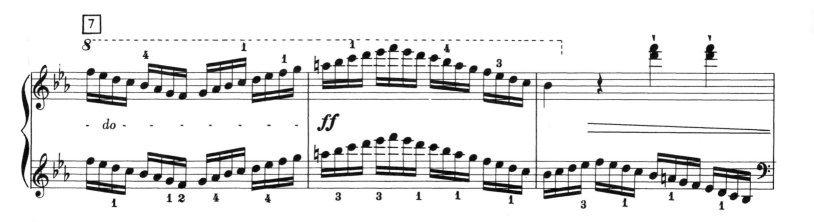

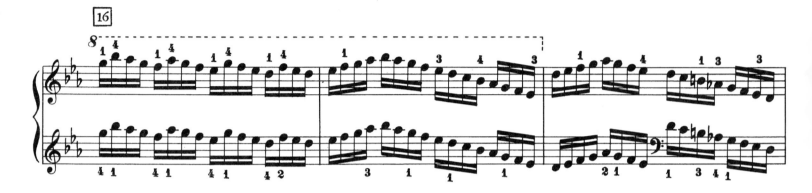

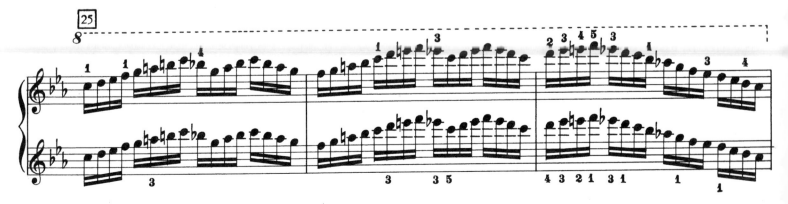

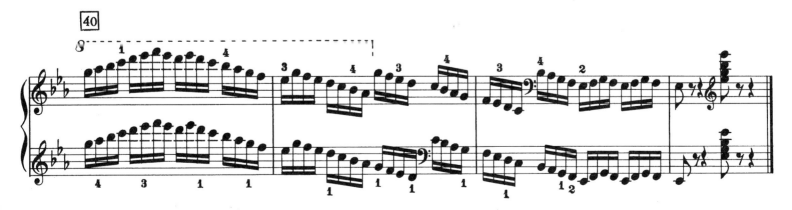

74

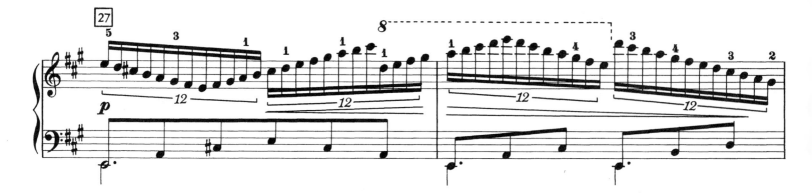

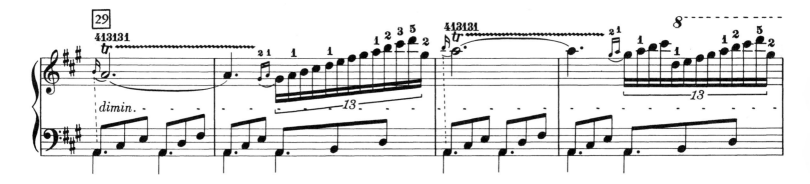

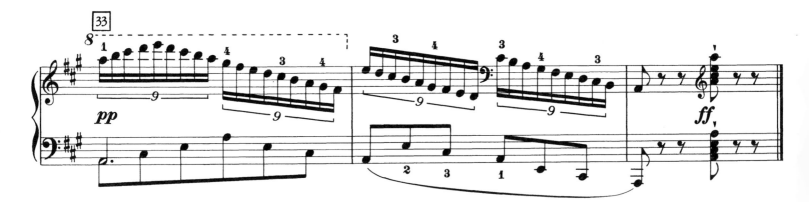

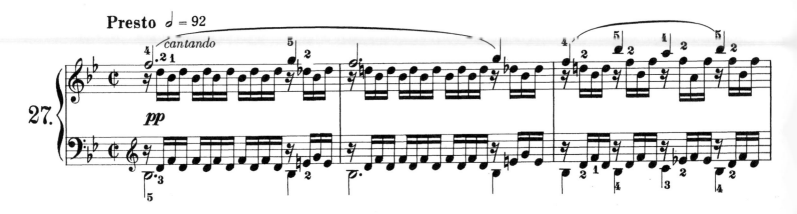

Molto Allegro ♩ = 100

29.

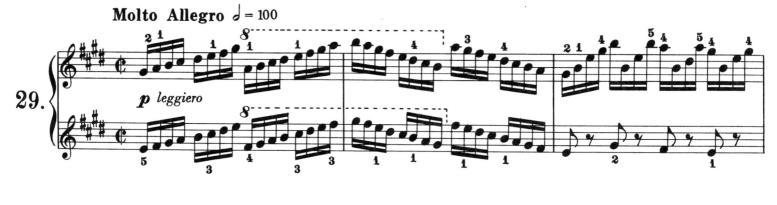

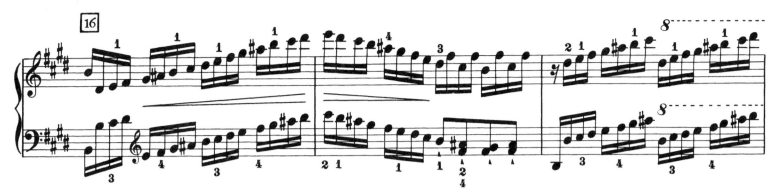

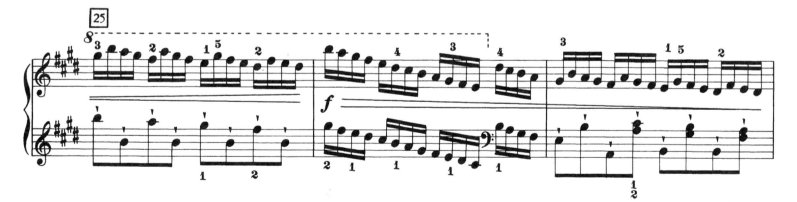

Presto volante ♩. = 69

30.

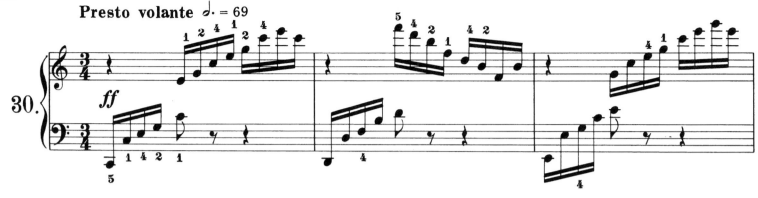

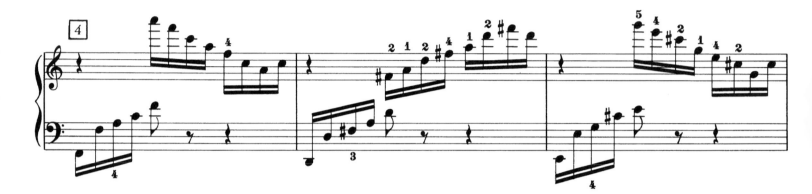

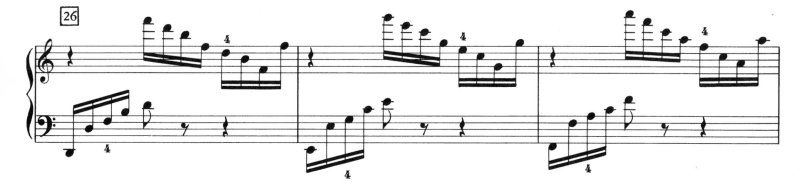

The School of Velocity

Book 4

Edited by
Willard A. Palmer

Carl Czerny Op. 299, Book 4

84

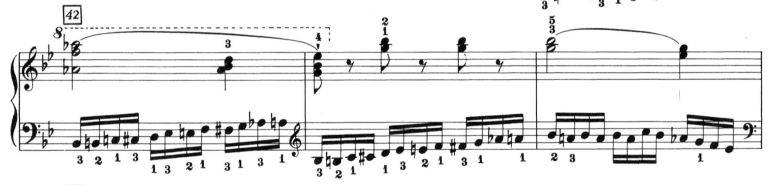

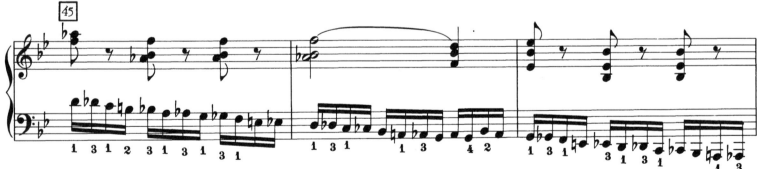

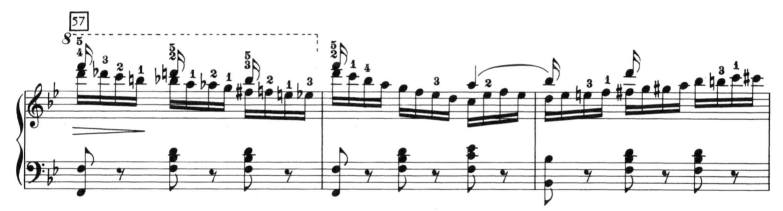

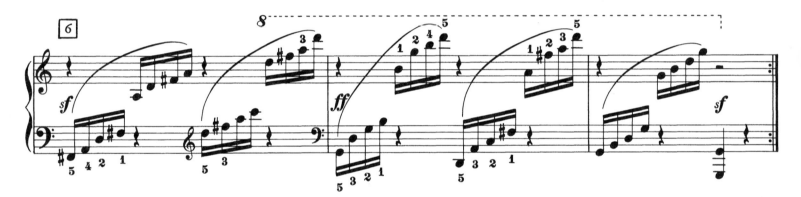

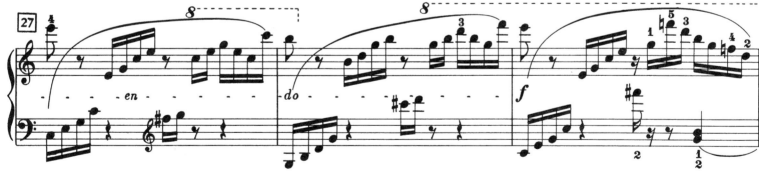

Molto Allegro e veloce ♩ = 138

33.

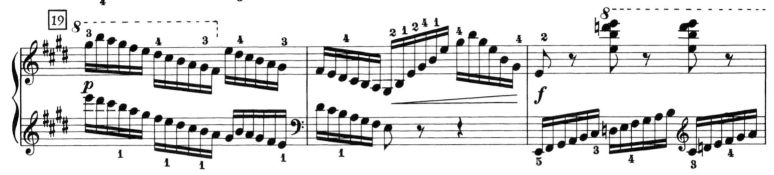

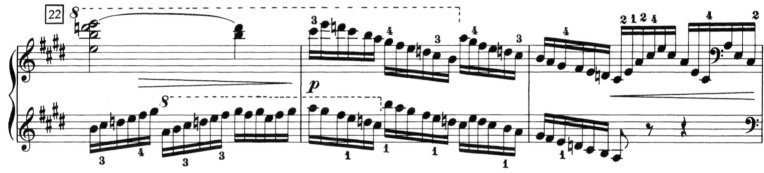

Allegro molto vivo ed energico ♩ = 88

34.

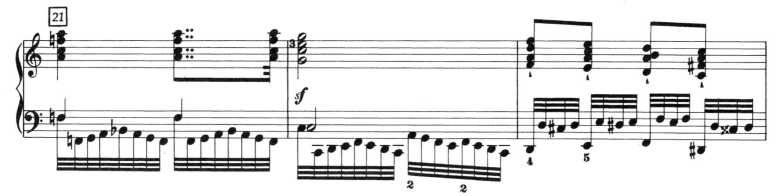

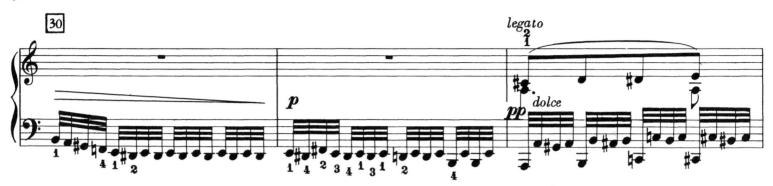

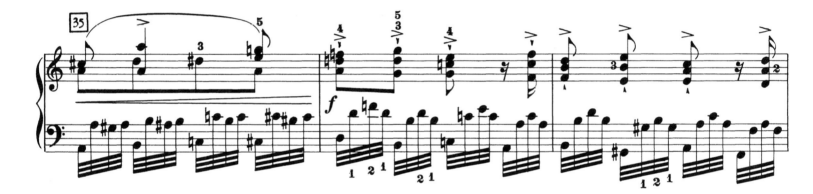

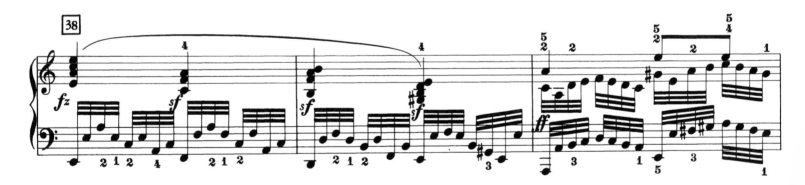

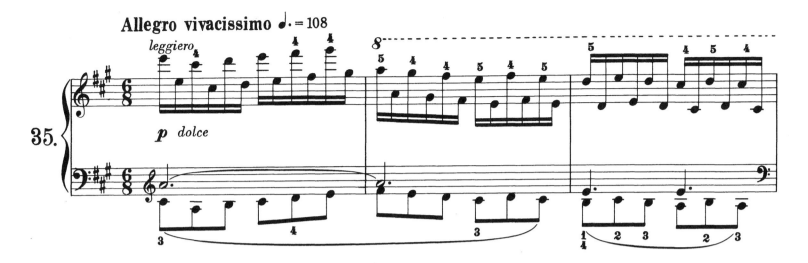

94

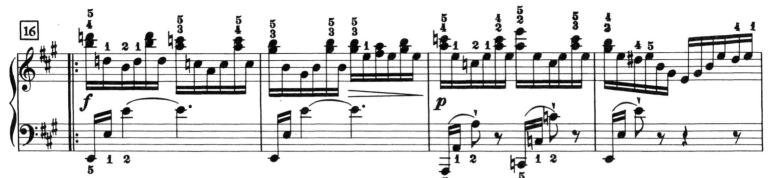

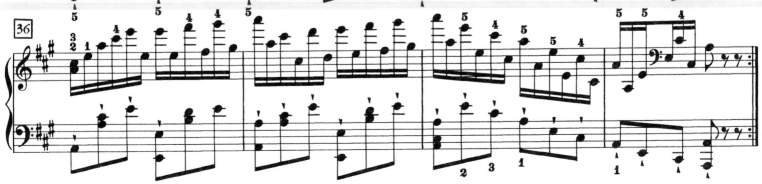

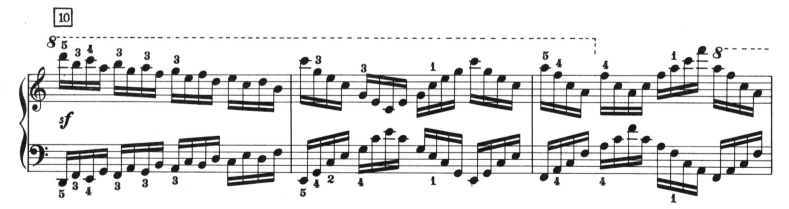

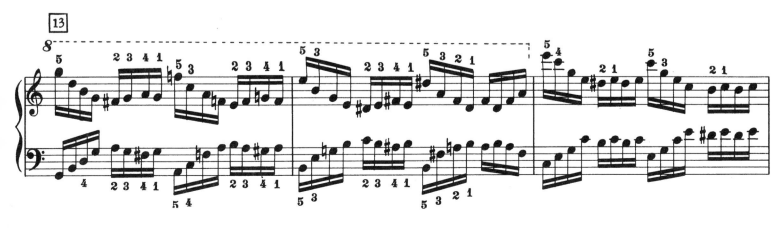

96

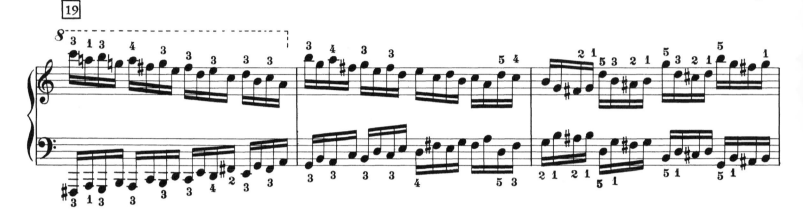

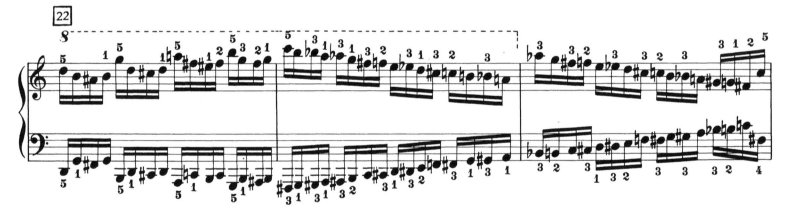

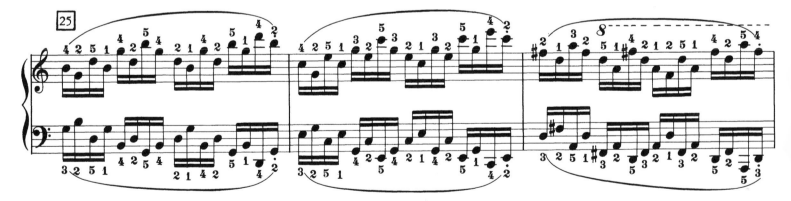

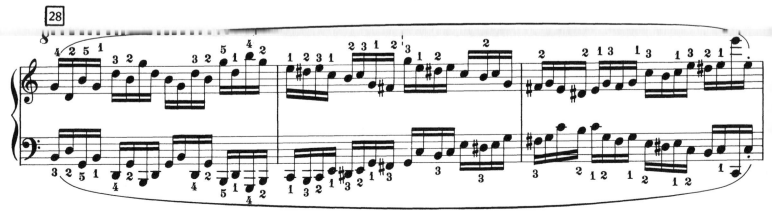

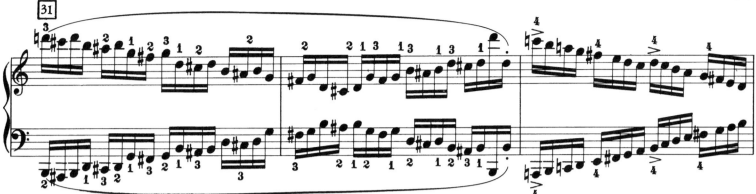

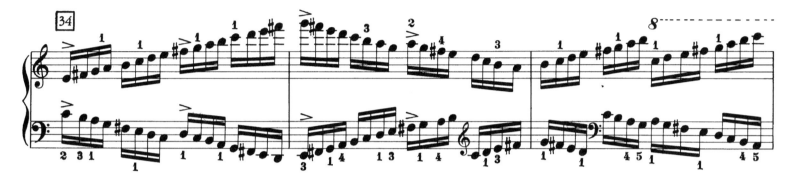

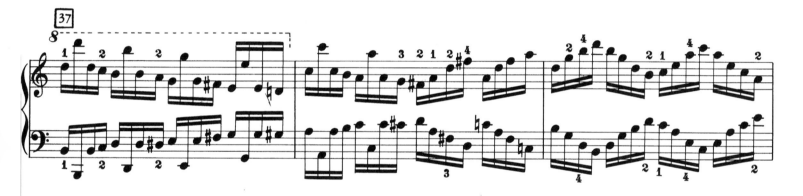

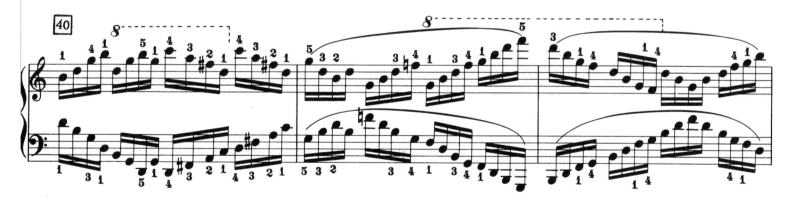

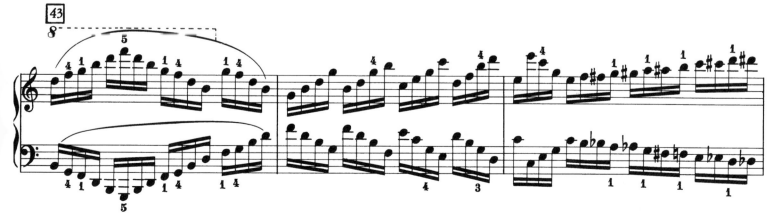

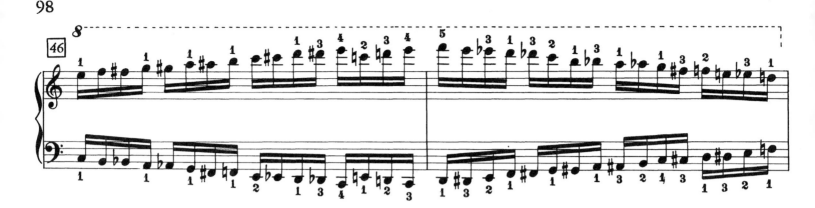

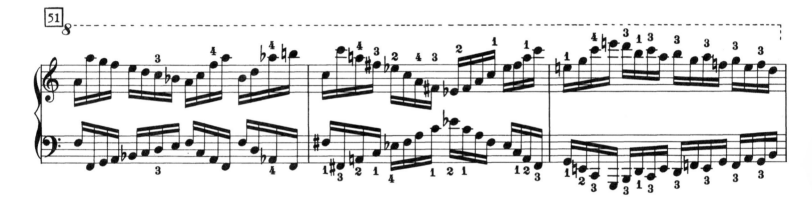

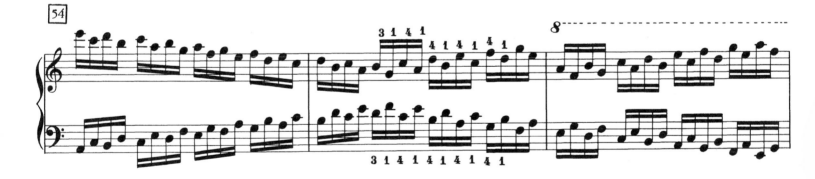

Molto Allegro e giocoso ♩ = 96

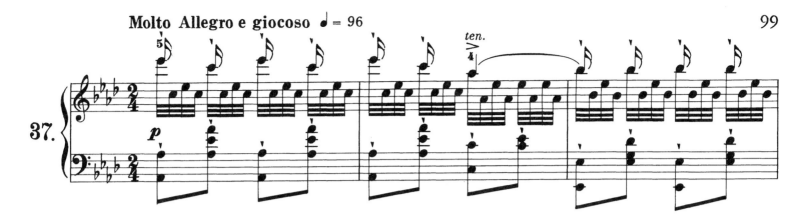

37.

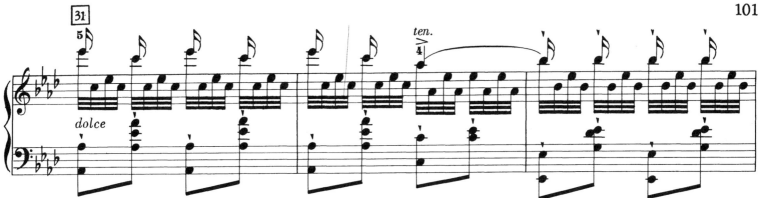

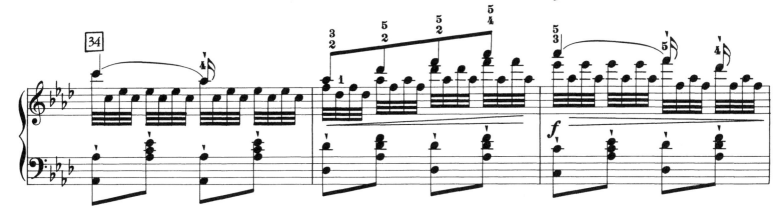

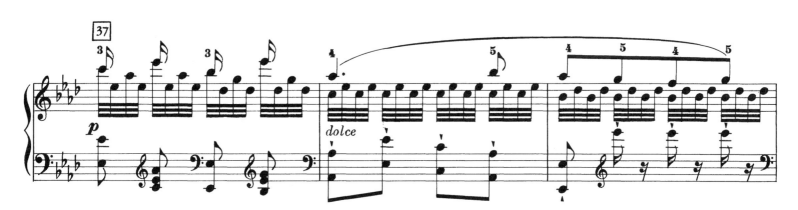

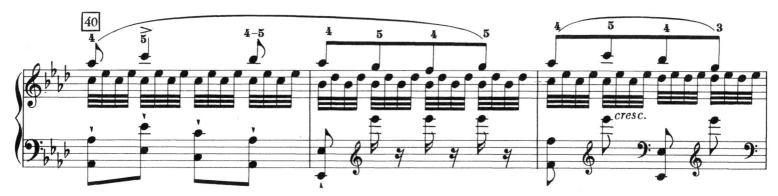

Molto Allègro, quasi presto ♩ = 84

38.

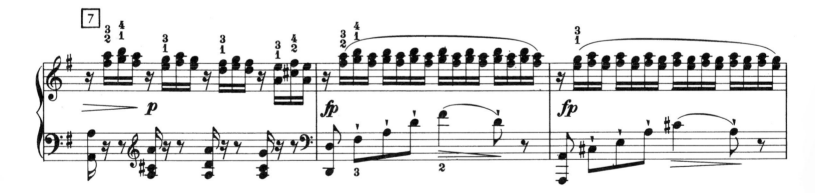

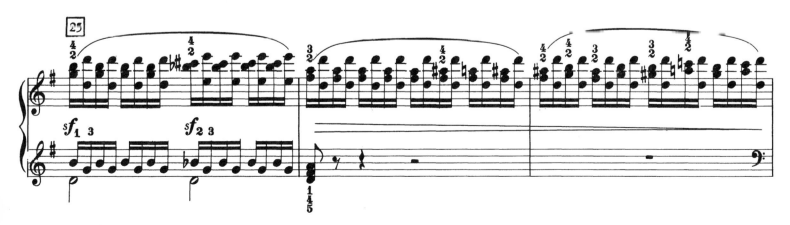

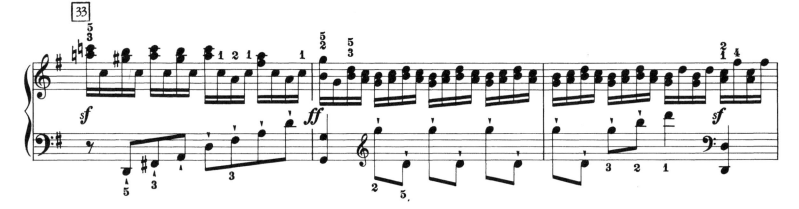

Presto (à la Galopade) ♩ = 104

39.

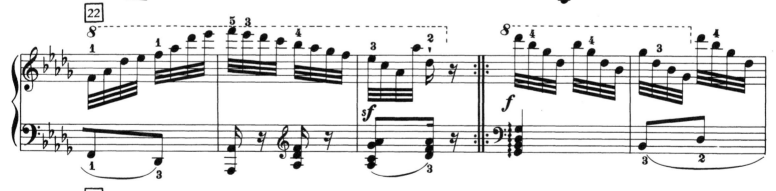

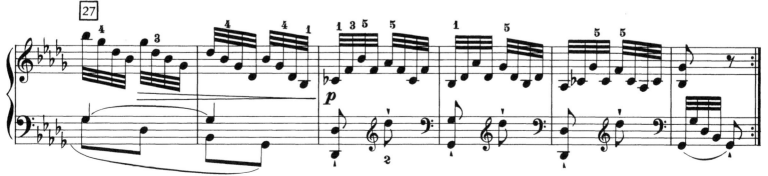

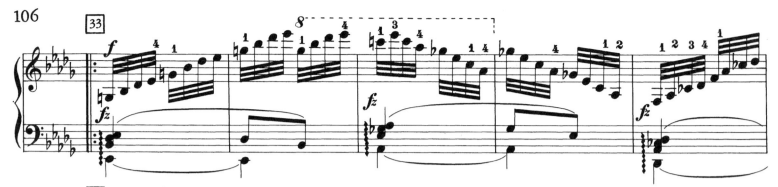

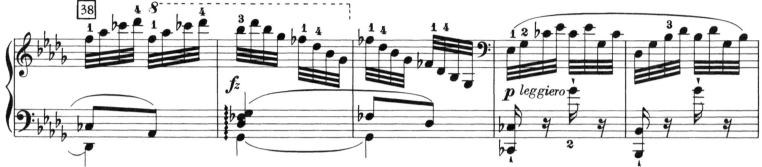

Allegrissimo, quasi presto ♩ = 120

40.

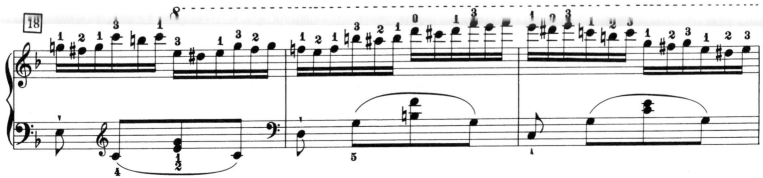

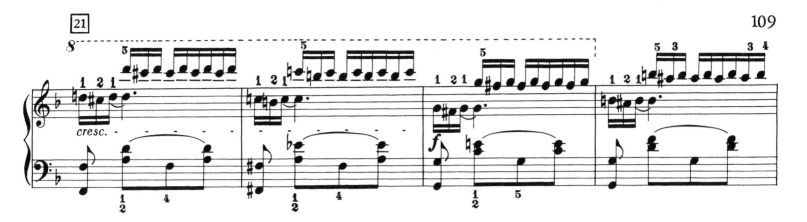

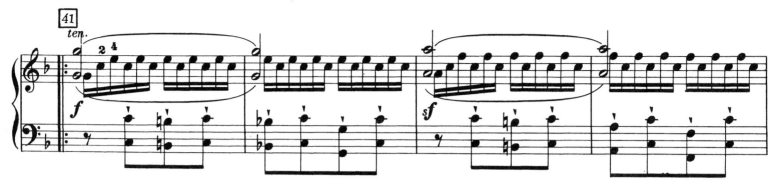

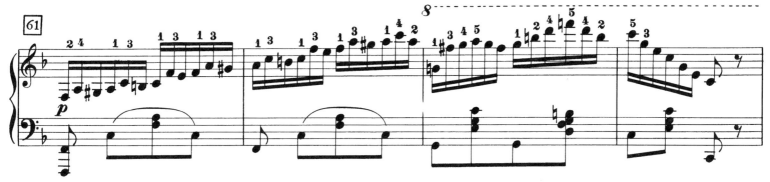

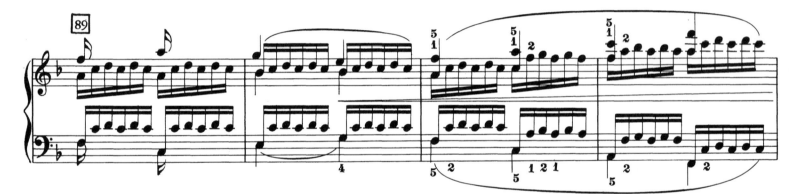

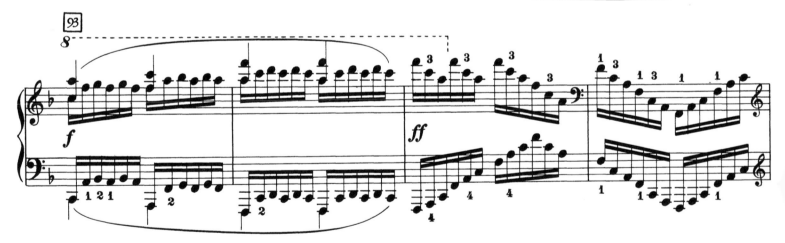

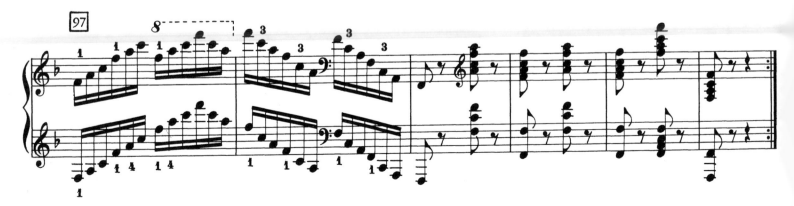